The Freedom of Christ

The Freedom of Christ

Sermons on Galatians

TIMOTHY MATTHEW SLEMMONS

Scripture quotations from the New Revised Standard Version of
the Bible are copyright © 1989 by the Division of Christian
Education of the National Council of the Churches of Christ in the
U.S.A., and are used by permission.

First edition

PRINTED IN THE UNITED STATES OF AMERICA
9 8 7 6 5 4 3 2 1

Library of Congress Cataloguing-in-Publication Data

Slemmons, Timothy Matthew
The Freedom of Christ: Sermons on Galatians / Timothy Matthew
Slemmons - 1st ed.

ISBN-13: 978-1508593348
ISBN-10: 1508593345

Grace to you and peace from God our Father and the Lord Jesus Christ, who gave himself for our sins to set us free from the present evil age, according to the will of our God and Father, to whom be the glory for ever and ever. Amen.

— Galatians 1:3-5

For freedom Christ has set us free. Stand firm, therefore, and do not submit again to a yoke of slavery.

—Galatians 5:1

For you were called to freedom, brothers and sisters; only do not use your freedom as an opportunity for self-indulgence, but through love become slaves to one another.

— Galatians 5:13

CONTENTS

Acknowledgements

There are many saints in New Jersey, some living and some now deceased, known to me through Princeton Theological Seminary, the New Brunswick Presbytery, and the First Presbyterian Church, Titusville, NJ, for whom I would like to express my deep appreciation. Indeed, they are too numerous to mention by name. But on this occasion, there is one for whom I am especially grateful: Phil Royer. Phil was a quiet, good-humored elder who was always on his feet to greet newcomers and visitors, to help the pastor in doing the requisite head count, and to suggest fresh ways and hopes of reaching the community with the Gospel. As one who was ever eager to take reminders of Sunday worship and the Christian life with him into the work week—the better to live out the faith—Phil showed a keen interest when I first placed some audio CDs of these sermons in the narthex as a form of outreach. Phil's encouragement has stuck with me through the last ten years for its rare warmth and genuine earnestness. It is in his memory that this modest series of Lenten sermons on Galatians, and on the sublime gospel of freedom, is humbly dedicated to the glory of God.

INTRODUCTION

This short series of sermons on Galatians, or rather a preliminary version thereof, was preached ten years ago over the Sundays of Lent in 2005 at the First Presbyterian Church, Titusville, NJ, in the first year of what turned out to be an extended interim pastorate that actually stretched to four years. Several factors prompted the selection of whole chapters for this series, including the nature of interim work itself, coupled with a renewed conviction that the preaching of the Word is God's ordained and preferred means of reforming the church, whether broadly at the denominational level or more narrowly within a particular congregation.

During this same period I was working out, in both theory and experimentation, a foray into the canonical zone untouched by the *Revised Common Lectionary* with a fourth year of lections, since published as *Year D*, with its emphasis on promoting the most comprehensive exposure to the canon possible and on giving priority to continuous and semi-continuous reading wherever feasible.[1] In the course of the design process, the Sundays in Lent seemed an opportune time to preach through a mid-length epistle using the *Westminster Directory*'s robust rule for reading one chapter per week.[2]

Other contextual factors bear mentioning in order to hopefully lend some sense of orientation to the reader. Allow me to enumerate them not so much in a prescriptive as an indicative mood, with the aim of simply documenting the priorities and influences informing the approach taken in this first year after my doctoral studies in homiletics. After the Word itself, of course, and a general, yet earnest resolution to labor within the expository tradition (broadly understood), the chief influence was that of Kierkegaard, who was the focus of my doctoral studies; that influence will be seen here

---

[1] Slemmons, *Year D: A Quadrennial Supplement to the Revised Common Lectionary* (Eugene, OR: Cascade Books, 2012).

[2] It actually calls for reading one chapter from each testament. See Bard Thompson, ed., *Liturgies of the Western Church* (Philadelphia: Fortress Press, 1961) 345-71, esp. 358.

not as one might expect, in a plethora of "indirect" third-person illustrations (per Craddock),[3] but in the attempt to differentiate between the existential stages in heuristic matters of interpretation, as well in the aim of prompting, encouraging, and drawing to consciousness the listener's interior conversation with the Holy Spirit. Moreover, one will encounter here the occasional run-on sentence, a stylistic taboo for modern preachers that, when meticulously smoothed over and carefully delivered, can nevertheless lend musicality, momentum, and motive force. Without presuming any basis whatsoever for comparison between these sermons and *Christian Discourses* or *Works of Love*, I nevertheless admit to having been shaped by the arresting and edifying beauty of such homiletical wonderworks, as will surely be more evident in aspiration here than in actual execution.

In a related vein, while inspired by Kierkegaard's (and Karl Barth's) dialectical method,[4] it seemed to me that the problems

---

[3] In my dissertation, "Toward a Penitential Homiletic: Authority and Direct Communication in Christian Proclamation," (Princeton Theological Seminary, PhD. diss., 2004), I critique Craddock's methodological misreading of Kierkegaard in *Overhearing the Gospel: Overhearing the Gospel: Preaching and Teaching the Faith to Persons Who Have Already Heard* (Nashville: Abingdon Press, 1979).

[4] See my *Groans of the Spirit: Homiletical Dialectics in an Age of Confusion* (Eugene, OR: Pickwick Publications, 2010).

besetting the church at large, both currently and for many generations, might well be characterized as an increasingly static dialectic between two prevailing dialectics, namely, between Hegelian synthesis (*both/and*) and Kierkegaardian ultimatum (*either/or*). Thus, if any sort of transformation were to be possible, a fresh and specifically homiletical dialectic was in order, one that could transcend this tension and do so in a way that is true to Scripture and a Reformed (ever reforming) theology of the Word, one that could "sow to the Spirit" (Gal 6:8) in bringing about both qualitative and quantitative change, both actual transformation and incremental progress. I cannot claim, by any stretch, to have invented *from/to* thinking about homiletical matters, since it has for twenty centuries run everywhere through the literature, sometimes meandering as an undercurrent and at other times erupting as a veritable geyser, but I do think at this stage it merits promotion to dialectical status.

In recent homiletics, one thinks of the purpose statement (Sidney Griedanus, Haddon Robinson), the function statement (Thomas Long), the anthropological study that informs the homiletics of Leonora Tubbs Tisdale, the trouble in need of a gracious solution in the problem solving approaches of Eugene Lowry and Paul Scott Wilson, and lively discussions of the purposes of preaching that seem very far indeed from any kind of consensus.[5] In previous generations, we encounter similar concerns in Harry Emerson Fosdick's insistence on pastoral relevance, Reu's thoroughly ecclesial and edifying understanding of the purpose of the sermon, and innumerable treatments of the aim of preaching in handbooks of sacred rhetoric. In each of these and in every generation, one is sooner or later reminded of the preacher's obligation to deal honestly and fairly with the current contextual situation: the state of the church at large or a congregation's worldview, a prevailing problem or a presenting need, as well as the desired outcome of the sermon, whether that is predominantly baptismal (awakening unto conversion and discipleship), Eucharistic (edifying and equipping for mission), or purely doxological. Personally, I find such a broadly Trinitarian paradigm most helpful when it comes to what I hope shall result from any given sermon. A more detailed account of this nascent teleology of preaching must await another occasion. Suffice it to say that what is needed is a dialectic that is genuinely (i.e., scripturally, spiritually, and eschatologically) progressive, yet free from the sanctimonious trappings that progressivism swiftly acquires when it is politicized and

---

[5] Jana Childers, ed., *Purposes of Preaching* (St. Louis, MO: Chalice Press, 2004).

secularized, that is, divorced from participation—
and faith!—in what the Triune God is doing in the
world.

Another influence evident in these sermons is
the history of the congregation itself: founded in
1844, with a rousing dedicatory sermon on
missions by Princeton professor Samuel Miller,[6] in
the environs of the first Great Awakening nearly a
century before that; poised on a virtual island
between the Raritan canal and the Delaware
River, the landscape around this "river church" in
New Brunswick Presbytery seemed to fairly
reverberate with the tones, cadences, and
concerns of the awakeners Theodorus
Frelinghuysen, Gilbert Tennent, and George
Whitefield. At the same time, with each new
theological issue to arise, the congregation
experienced many of the same tensions and
concerns other congregations were undergoing,
but with the heightened sense of responsibility to
ever-present reminders of her theological and
ecclesial heritage. This became something of a
common denominator between preacher and
congregation, for Tennent's work had become an
interest of mine, especially as I came away from
my Kierkegaard studies with questions regarding
the homiletical aim of awakening in particular,

---

[6] Samuel Miller, "The Glory of the Gospel: A Sermon on
1Timothy 1:11", ed. Timothy Matthew Slemmons (Titusville, NJ:
First Presbyterian Church, 2005).

and the uneasy sense that both Kierkegaard and Tennent, though judged by many to be overly harsh and strident, nevertheless had some very legitimate concerns about the integrity of the ministry (and even specific ministers) in their respective times and places, a concern that is borne out in both testaments of the Bible as well as in the state of the church today. Thus, these sermons were preached at a time with a desire to both honor and set the stage for the awakening potential of the preached Word and to do so in such a way that refined the integrity of the congregation's witness while avoiding any needless divisions.

As for the form of these sermons, the approach taken here is less explicitly explicative, so to speak, and more a matter of what I would call *reiterative exposition*. In many ways, it is the same principle, or wager, at work in *Year D*, that is, less a matter of the rhetorical structure of an argument, and more one of simply providing a fresh framework in which the Word may do its work, or from which it may be uttered and heard and believed anew. Since these sermons were preached, I have found the term "sense units"—as suggested by Ronald J. Allen and Gilbert Bartholomew[7]—the best description of the divisions of the text, as these

---

[7] Ronald J. Allen and Gilbert Bartholomew, *Preaching Verse By Verse* (Louisville: Westminster John Knox Press, 2000).

lend structure to the sermon and line up with one another, as pieces in a puzzle, so as to reveal the spiritual logic that connects them.

Finally, the focus of each of these sermons is fixed on the claims Paul is making that, to my mind, so far surpass all others that they draw attention to themselves by way of what may seem like hyperbole (if we were to fall victim to the quantitative fallacy and call them merely "big ideas"), but is in fact pure, true, revelatory, categorical language characteristic of what Kierkegaard and Barth called the "infinite qualitative difference." These, what at the risk of being called "absolutist" I would call, "absolutes" are hopefully made clear in the sermon titles themselves: "No Other Gospel," "The Freedom of Christ: It is No Longer I," "Not Unity in Diversity, But Unity in Christ," "Born According to the Spirit," "The Only Thing That Counts," "Everything!" In each case, the focus is on the essential, unique, and irreplaceable gospel: the gospel of human freedom in Christ and ultimately the freedom of the Christ who, for the sake of freedom, has set us free.

This is, I believe, the grand theme of Galatians and is arguably the best way of phrasing the gospel according to Paul. What is more, preaching and hearing the gospel as essentially a matter of eternal freedom (even if it appears restrictive in temporality) seems to me especially urgent at this time, with the alarming rise of leftist statism on the one hand and a new conservative libertarianism on the other; the one threatening to strip people of basic human and civil freedoms for the sake of a false and fleeting security supposedly "guaranteed" by a smothering state, and the other championing purely individualistic freedom from oppressive control, restriction, and taxation in order to safeguard the political right to, aside from many good things, indulge in any number of spiritually enslaving and morally self-destructive "works of the flesh" (Gal 5:16-21). Amidst such threats and tensions, there is only one guarantor of unity, identity, peace, and freedom; only one gospel that truly signals good news. It is in the service of this One, Jesus Christ, and his gospel, the gospel concerning him, that these sermons were preached and are now, once again, released into the world.

TMS
"Mamre"
Dubuque, IA
First Sunday of Lent, AD 2015

The Freedom of Christ

Sermons on Galatians

No Other Gospel
(Galatians 1:1-24)

[First Sunday of Lent, *February 13, 2005*]

PRAYER

Holy God, you are love! Holy Love, you are God, revealed in Jesus Christ who gave himself for our sins, to set us free from the present evil age! Now, O God, let your Spirit descend here, descend and remain; bring to mind once more the truth we have heard and enliven the proclamation of the faith, that we may each receive a fresh revelation of your gospel of freedom, the freedom that emerges when we take obedience to heart. Amen.

1. Introduction

An apostle, by definition, is one who is sent, commissioned by a superior to perform a particular task, like an ambassador, a delegate, a representative. In the case of Christian scripture and the apostolic church, that superior who commissions and sends is the invisible Triune God: God the Father, God the Son, God the Holy Spirit. The process of God's commissioning and sending, however, involves those human agents whom God has similarly called and sent, involves them in a process of something known as apostolic succession, ordination, setting certain people apart to fulfill a particular function, and because human apostles and commissioners are *visibly* involved in what the *invisible* God is working to bring about in human affairs, it is all too easy to overlook or forget God's role in the whole process.

Paul, thus begins his most combative letter, to a cluster of churches in Galatia, in what is today central Turkey, by reminding them of the all important distinction between God's initiative and human initiative, between God's authority and human authority, because there is "an infinite qualitative difference."

> Paul an apostle — sent neither by human commission nor from human authorities, but through Jesus Christ and God the Father,

> who raised him from the dead — and all the
> members of God's family who are with me,
> To the churches of Galatia: Grace to you and
> peace from God our Father and the Lord
> Jesus Christ ... (1:1-3).

But the apostle does not to beat around the
bush. Even while he is still issuing his diplomatic
greeting he states his reason for writing: the
Galatians have abandoned the true gospel, and
before he has finished saying, "Hello," he
reiterates it for them as clearly as possible. This
Jesus Christ is the one ...

> who gave himself for our sins to set us free
> from the present evil age, according to the
> will of our God and Father, to whom be the
> glory forever and ever. Amen. (1:4-5)

There it is, like John 3:16, the gospel in a
nutshell: *Jesus Christ has given himself for our sins to
set us free from the present evil age.*

2. Apostolic authority rests on the revelation itself
What is the basis of Paul's authority? What is the
nature of *anyone's* authority, for that matter? Put as
simply as possible: authority from a Christian
point of view derives from *the content of the
revelation*. What is it that God has revealed to be
the good news? The gospel!

The one who preaches, teaches, speaks, acts with authority, is the one who holds to the gospel! Freedom from sin, freedom in Christ, freedom, not to participate in or partake of evil things, but freedom from the present evil age. Those who announce, show, tell, embody, or exemplify, in their manner of thinking, speaking, living, and enacting, this good news concerning Jesus Christ, this freedom in Christ, have true authority, and their authority remains true as long as they do not alter the good news for convenience, or pervert it based on societal expectations, or abandon it under peer pressure, political correctness, or persecution. But this is exactly what had happened with the Galatian churches.

> I am astonished that you are so quickly deserting the one who called you in the grace of Christ and are turning to a different gospel—not that there is another gospel, but there are some who are confusing you and want to pervert the gospel of Christ. But even if we or an angel from heaven should proclaim to you a gospel contrary to what we proclaimed to you, let that one be accursed! As we have said before, so now I repeat, if anyone proclaims to you a gospel contrary to what you received, let that one be accursed! (1:6-9)

What has happened, is that *some* Jews — *some!* — who did not believe the gospel of grace and could not abide by the freedom in Christ had followed Paul from Jerusalem, and were trying to revise his teaching, to collapse grace back into law, telling the Gentile believers that if they want to be Christians, they must first become Jews, if they wanted to be saved, they must first fulfill the law, and the particular law in question was that the men among them must be circumcised.

3. *Circumcision addressed and applied*

As you know, this medical procedure which is so common today, was originally not a law, but a sign of God's covenant with Abraham, one that, outwardly involved only the males, yet even as far back as Deuteronomy, some seventeen centuries before Paul, Moses said:

> Circumcise, then, the foreskin *of your heart*, and do not be stubborn any longer (Deut 10:16).

In other words, when it comes to obeying the law, obedience is not to be offered grudgingly, as though the law was intended to be a burden, but *you have got to put your heart into it*. In the case of circumcision, outward forms of mutilation and scarification are meaningless, and even cruel, and

7

there are cultures today that practice such cruelty on little girls. But the *outward* way is not the way to include the females among us! This is *not* what the Lord intends!

Obedience and devotion to God is *not* about cosmetic surgery, which today is all the rage, it is *not* about an outward covering, like an overcoat, or like a veil that lies over the minds of those who read the books of Moses which they do not understand. In 2Corinthians, Paul writes of those whose minds, he says, are hardened, like the stone tablets of the law; the law that performed the ministry, not of justification, but of condemnation; the law that brought not life but death:

> But their minds were hardened. Indeed, to this very day, when they hear the reading of the old covenant, that same veil is still there, since only in Christ is it set aside. Indeed, to this very day whenever Moses is read, a veil lies over their minds; but when one turns to the Lord, the veil is removed. Now the Lord is the Spirit, and where the Spirit of the Lord is, there is freedom" (2Cor 3:14-17).

Freedom! Christian freedom! This is not only the great theme of Galatians, it is essential to our understanding of the one and only gospel! True devotion to God, devotion that seeks *his* glory, is discovered where *obedience* is freely chosen, where obedience and freedom make contact. It sounds like a contradiction to the earthly mind, to the hardened, carnal mind. But this is the true point of contact between your spirit and the Spirit of the Lord!

Now if I were you, sitting where you are sitting right now, I would silently—so that neither the preacher nor your neighbor knows what you are doing—let my thoughts wander from the sermon itself, wander in the direction of the LORD, and say, "LORD, as I sit here in your presence, and despite the fact that I don't even quite understand this strange metaphor or the full implications of what I am asking, I nevertheless ask you to please circumcise my heart in this very moment. Please remove any and all hardness or callousness that may be keeping me in the dark. As I turn my thoughts to you, Lord Jesus, let the veil be removed, and in seeking your face, let me too receive the revelation, let me too begin to enjoy the eternal light, let me too begin to thrill, either anew or for the very first time, at the knowledge of your personal nearness to me, and help me to remain in and return frequently to this boundless space in which I am able to reach up to you in an intimate, personal way." Friend, if you will do this, then you will soon discover there is nothing you want more than to please the LORD above all. Thus, in this same frame of mind, Paul asks:

> Am I now seeking human approval, or God's
> approval? Or am I trying to please people? If
> I were still pleasing people, I would not be a
> servant of Christ (Gal 1:10).

Now, having gone inward for a moment, having
marked that interior space as your meeting place
with the Lord, remember Paul's assurance that he
did not whip up this gospel in his own
imagination. He will spend the better part of this
chapter and the next one, insisting that his contact
with the other apostles was quite limited, and that,
while they acknowledged and verified the gospel
that he preached—*and there is no other gospel!*—
they themselves did not teach it to him.

> For I want you to know ... that the gospel
> that was proclaimed by me is not of human
> origin; for I did not receive it from a human
> source, nor was I taught it, but I received it
> through a revelation of Jesus Christ (1:11-12).

4. Conversion discussed and applied

Paul is talking about his conversion, resulting
from a powerful heavenly vision of the risen
Christ, who called out to him from heaven, not
only with a commission, but with compassion:

> "Saul, Saul, why are you persecuting me? It
> hurts you to kick against the goads. ... But get

up and stand on your feet; for I have appeared to you for this purpose, to appoint you to serve and testify to the things in which you have seen me and to those in which I will appear to you. I will rescue you from your people and from the Gentiles—to whom I am sending you to open their eyes so that they may turn from darkness to light and from the power of Satan to God, so that they may receive forgiveness of sins and a place among those who are sanctified by faith in me" (Acts 26:14-18).

The Lord's word to Paul is no less a word to you, not that the Lord wants or needs another Paul, or someone to walk precisely in the footsteps of Paul, but that he wants you to be *you*, to be your *best* you, and you only hurt yourself if you resist his will for you. Not only that, but, if you resist his will, you stand to lose out on the blessed mission and the very purpose for which God has created you. This is why we speak of conversion, or repentance, as a turning, a turning to Christ.

I know there are many folks who, when they hear the words *repentance* and *conversion*, immediately put their defenses up, as though it were really something threatening. Thus, the covering, the veil, the protective overcoat, the hard exterior goes back up and they hide inside. But when we think of conversion as a *turning*, it really is quite a simple thing, nothing terribly threatening at all.

Think of it this way. Which one of you, if you got in your car to go the grocery store, would arrive there if, when you got behind the wheel, you determined not to touch or use the steering wheel. You put your key in the ignition, you put the car in gear, you step on the gas, but you refuse to have anything to do with the steering wheel. Crash! I dare say you would not get far. I doubt very much if I could even make the relatively straight shot from the church down to the park if I did not use the wheel.

Now there are some who, in the life of faith are pretty much right on course. They are going on the best route, making good progress, knowing pretty much where they are going. But even these people have to turn the wheel, albeit slightly, yet more or less constantly, just to stay on the road. Then there are others, like those whose testimonies we hear from time to time; those who wake up one day, realize they are on the wrong road, going the wrong direction, heading to the wrong destination altogether. For them, the turning, the conversion that is needed is 180 degrees!

In a sense, conversion is like that. It really is a process that requires our constant attention. Sometimes things are going so well, you can *almost* take your hands off the wheel and still manage to stay on the road (but I still would not advise it), like when you are driving across the state of Iowa. Sometimes you need to turn more often, as when you are driving along the jagged coastline. Sometimes you are so lost, you have to turn around and go the opposite direction. But sometimes, even when you are on the more or less direct road to Damascus, heading for a street called Straight, even when you finish your journey without changing your geographical direction, you still have to have someone knock you off your horse and tell you that you, though you can keep on heading to Damascus, you must now do so as a whole new person. So begins Paul's testimony of his own radical turning, which is less an "about face" than it is a turning or a transformation into an entirely new creation:

> You have heard, no doubt, of my earlier life in Judaism. I was violently persecuting the church of God and was trying to destroy it. I advanced in Judaism beyond many among my people of the same age, for I was far more zealous for the traditions of my ancestors. But when God, who had set me apart before I was born and called me through his grace, was pleased to reveal his Son to me, so that I might proclaim him among the Gentiles, I did not confer with any human being, nor

did I go up to Jerusalem to those who were already apostles before me, but I went away at once into Arabia, and afterwards I returned to Damascus.

Then after three years I did go up to Jerusalem to visit Cephas and stayed with him fifteen days; but I did not see any other apostle except James the Lord's brother. In what I am writing to you, before God, I do not lie! Then I went into the regions of Syria and Cilicia, and I was still unknown by sight to the churches of Judea that are in Christ; they only heard it said, "The one who formerly was persecuting us is now proclaiming the faith he once tried to destroy." And they glorified God because of me (Gal 1:13-24).

This Paul, who now sits at the feet of the risen Savior, learning from him, rethinking all he—the star student—had once learned of Judaism at the feet of Gamaliel, reexamining the law of Moses now fully revealed in the light of Christ; Paul, as he contemplates his Savior and walks with him in the silence of the Arabian desert, as he stands in a strained, distant fellowship with the other apostles, differentiated from, yet in absolute solidarity of purpose with, Peter, James, and John, those before whom his own personal history and the intervention of the Lord have brought him to absolute humility—this Paul is now so completely contrary to the character of the fire-breathing Saul, who once imprisoned the members of the earthly church and even supervised the stoning of Stephen; Paul is so completely contrary to his prior nature, to Saul, that now, for him, the earthly church itself becomes an outpost of heaven, fulfilling the words of Jesus, where he said: "there will be more joy in heaven over one sinner who repents than over ninety-nine righteous persons who need no repentance" (Luke 15:7).

5. *Conclusion*

O let there be a turning, a fresh turning to freedom and joy among us! Let God be so glorified today and in the days to come as you take to heart, and take your part in, this new season of turning, of correcting your steering, of guiding your conveyances into the freedom we have in Christ, into the path of the one true gospel, into the ancient way of peace.

Let obedience emerge in, and merge into, freedom. Let your spirit be refreshed by the Spirit of God, as you realize that Christian authority and leadership are best exercised when we hold fast to the gospel revelation. For those commissioned to serve this congregation, and *you*, the local missionaries who are sent out through these doors each Sunday, are to go and serve in the apostolic tradition, and are therefore called to steer a straight course, not only for yourselves and your families, but for this family of faith.

Yes, you, whoever you are, whatever the Lord is calling you to do: let your steering, your turning, likewise be true to the one true gospel, the gospel of freedom in Christ, freedom from the present evil age; for there is no other gospel than this.

The Freedom of Christ: It is No Longer I
(Galatians 2:1-21)

[Second Sunday of Lent, *February 13, 2005*]

PRAYER

You have claimed us from the beginning, O God, and established your claim with the cross of Christ. Now help us to humbly bow and submit to your claim, to offer to you all our unresolved questions and concerns, all our fruitless struggles and strivings, all our self-directed labors and loves, whether legal or illicit, sinful or selfish, to surrender them, along with ourselves, to you as we count everything as loss for the sake of knowing Christ, for the sake of seeing everything in the light of his death for us, for the sake of our dying with him, dying to the present evil age, that each may truly say of his or her own life, "It is now no longer I."

We hear a lot about freedom these days. Perhaps today especially—on Washington's birthday, worshiping where we are, landlocked between the Delaware River and Washington's Crossing State Park, with another President George W. talking about freedom, aspiring to take democracy to the oppressed and tyrannized parts of the globe—we are likely to have freedom on the brain, freedom on the tongue, freedom finding expression in lots of noble and sometimes ignoble ways.

The letter to the Galatians is a letter about freedom, but the freedom in question is not primarily freedom in relation to human forms of government, political tyrants, economic systems, and social customs, though it certainly does have its implications, and makes its influence felt, in these spheres of life. The freedom with which the apostle is concerned is not the sort of freedom you have by virtue of your birth in, or your immigration to, a free country, the sort of freedom that ends when you die and you have to surrender your passport, your driver's license, and your Social Security card. Without wishing to diminish the enormous value of the temporal freedoms with which we are blessed, *the freedom of Christ* is an altogether different, infinitely higher, sort of freedom; it is *eternal* freedom, the sort of freedom that, in a certain sense, only those who have died, only those who have been crucified with Christ, can fully enjoy.

In Chapter One of Galatians, we learned that there is only one gospel, none other than the good news that the Lord Jesus Christ, the Son of God, gave himself for our sins to set us free from the present evil age. The apostle, who had once gone by the name of Saul of Tarsus, writes to the Galatians about how he himself was first set free, so free that he who had once tried to destroy the church, had emerged at the Syrian end of his straight course for destruction as a completely different person, with a whole new purpose, a whole new perspective on his Hebrew faith, a whole new understanding of the scriptures, a whole new living relationship with his holy God, and even a whole new name: Paul. We learned that the blinding heavenly light, that is, the One who spoke from it: Jesus, had revealed the one true gospel to him with such power and clarity, that he did not need any human teacher to give him a crash course in Christianity. His own crashing to the ground, his three days in the darkness, his baptism by Ananias of Damascus, his three years in Damascus and in the deserts of Arabia, his travels in Syria and Cilicia—all of these went into his re-education in the school of freedom, such that even a fortnight with Peter, and a meeting in Jerusalem with James the brother of Jesus, did not, he says, alter the gospel he received in any way. Rather, they confirmed it. With Saul now effectively dead and buried, Paul went ahead and preached and taught and argued for freedom in Christ for fourteen years after his conversion, and the church was amazed that their arch enemy was now their strongest proponent, and they gave glory to God!

One might think that, even for an apostle like Paul, there would arise times of self-doubt, times when he wondered whether his new perspective amounted to a change that was too radical, when he worried that his own weakness might lead him astray, and that he might lead others astray with false teaching. Not a bit of it! In fact, doubt is no characteristic of an apostle; but faith is! The apostle operates *entirely* in the sphere of faith! And what finally led Paul to Jerusalem again, more than a decade later, was not any self-doubt, but another revelation: a revelation and faith!

> Then after fourteen years I went up again to Jerusalem with Barnabas, taking Titus along with me. I went up in response to a revelation. Then I laid before them (though only in a private meeting with the acknowledged leaders) the gospel that I proclaim among the Gentiles, in order to make sure that I was not running, or had not run, in vain (2:1-2).

Again the gospel is confirmed, not only in terms of its objective facts, but in terms of the subject of human life itself, in terms of the most concrete, earthy, personal circumstances imaginable.

> But even Titus, who was with me, was not compelled to be circumcised, though he was a Greek. ... And from those who were supposed to be acknowledged leaders (what they actually were makes no difference to me; God shows no partiality)—those leaders contributed nothing to me. On the contrary, when they saw that I had been entrusted with the gospel for the uncircumcised, just as Peter had been entrusted with the gospel for the circumcised (for he who worked through Peter making him an apostle to the circumcised also worked through me in sending me to the Gentiles), and when James and Cephas and John, who were acknowledged pillars, recognized the grace that had been given to me, they gave to Barnabas and me the right hand of fellowship, agreeing that we should go to the Gentiles and they to the circumcised. They asked only one thing, that we remember the poor, which was actually what I was eager to do (2:2, 6-10).

Here you see those derived implications, the *by-products* of the freedom of Christ. First, the apostles all agree that giving generously to the poor is indisputably an identifying mark of Christian love, showing not only love for the poor as Jesus did, but also *economic freedom*, freedom from the worry that you will not have enough for yourself, freedom that springs from "seeking first the kingdom of God and his righteousness," and the knowledge that if you do this, God will surely give you everything else you need as well (Matt 6:25-34). The Christian is one who says, "It is no longer I for whom I am concerned." Second, Titus, an uncircumcised Greek, is free from the legal demands and the social expectations of the Hebrew *torah* that would require him to undergo circumcision, to make him look Jewish, in the locker room or the gymnasium or the public baths, at least.

When it comes to the freedom of Christ, however, these social and ethical matters are *evidence* of this freedom, they are good works born of this freedom, but they are *not* the freedom itself!

Paul did not let his faith flag. At every point, *the freedom of Christ* was in the front of his mind as he made every decision. Even when, on another occasion, Paul took Timothy "and had him circumcised because of the Jews who were in those places," who "all knew that his father was a

Greek" (Acts 16:3), even then, it was for the advance of the gospel among the Jews who knew that Timothy's mother was a Jew (16:2), it was for gaining an entrée with them that Paul had him circumcised.

A double-standard? Not at all! It was a decision made within the bounds of freedom, consistent with Timothy's Jewish heritage, and for the sake of giving the gospel an opportunity among the Jews that it would otherwise not have had. The apostle, who in faith has become all things to all people, that he might by all means save some (1Cor 9:22), says in the Spirit, "Some judge one day to be better than another, while others judge all days to be alike. *Let all be fully convinced in their own minds.* Those who observe the day, observe it in honor of the Lord. Also those who eat, eat in honor of the Lord, since they give thanks to God; while those who abstain, abstain in honor of the Lord and give thanks to God" (Rom 14:5-6). "The faith that you have, have as your own conviction before God" (14:22a). "We do not live to ourselves, and we do not die to ourselves. If we live, we live to the Lord, and if we die, we die to the Lord; so then, whether we live or whether we die, we belong to the Lord" (Rom 14:7-8).

This is precisely the stance, the posture, of the one who is truly free in Christ, and far more importantly, the one in whom Christ is free! Saul the Pharisee is dead. He has *already* died to the Lord. But Paul is already eternally *alive* to the Lord. And even though some spies will sneak in among his fellows, trying to catch him in a double standard, nevertheless, because of the death of Saul, there is no double-mindedness to be detected.

> But because of false believers secretly brought in, who slipped in to spy on the freedom we have in Christ Jesus, so that they might enslave us — we did not submit to them even for a moment, so that the truth of the gospel might always remain with you (Gal 2:4-5).

The truth of the gospel, the freedom in Christ, must be *consistently* presented as freedom: freedom gained by dying to sin and to the law. Sadly, it seems, Cephas (Cephas being a Hebrew nickname for Peter, especially when he is timid before his Jewish critics) and even Barnabas the Encourager—these two apostles lapse for a moment into a real double-standard, lapse, that is, out of the gospel of freedom and into the old bondage to the law and social custom. For Cephas felt free enough to eat with the Greeks for a time, until those who legalistically insisted that circumcision be imposed on the Greeks, showed up, and then he drew back. Paul writes:

> But when Cephas came to Antioch, I
> opposed him to his face, because he stood
> self-condemned; for until certain people
> came from James, he used to eat with the
> Gentiles. But after they came, he drew back
> and kept himself separate for fear of the
> circumcision faction. And the other Jews
> joined him in this hypocrisy, so that even
> Barnabas was led astray by their hypocrisy.
> But when I saw that they were not acting
> consistently with the truth of the gospel, I
> said to Cephas before them all, "If you,
> though a Jew, live like a Gentile and not like
> a Jew, how can you compel the Gentiles to
> live like Jews? We ourselves are Jews by birth
> and not Gentile sinners; yet we know that a
> person is justified not by the works of the law
> but through faith in Jesus Christ." (2:15-16a)

Here again, faith is far beyond the reach of
anyone who has been able to climb the ladder of
the law without slipping. And who might that be,
you ask? I would not venture a guess. But even if
we *could* identify someone, besides Jesus, who had
reached the top rung, the highest state of ethical
perfection, what would that prove? Only that one
cannot reach faith by that means; only that the
ethical ladder of the law gets you so high and no
higher, certainly never high enough to storm the

gates of heaven. No, such a balancing act atop the ladder of perfection is not faith, and it certainly is not freedom, for in such a precarious state, one cannot afford to move at all, much less make a false move. But,

> we have come to believe in Christ Jesus, so that we might be justified by faith in Christ, and not by doing the works of the law, because no one will be justified by the works of the law. But if, in our effort to be justified in Christ, we ourselves have been found to be sinners, is Christ then a servant of sin? Certainly not! But if I build up again the very things that I once tore down, then I demonstrate that I am a transgressor (2:16-18).

The law itself, at least in its first and second uses, is my accuser, convicting me of sin. But when I am honest, admitting that I am a sinner, when I learn to stand with Christ the Lamb, to stand as one slain, as one who is already dead, executed according to the law, then I too am able to rise with Christ, with Christ no longer kept at arm's length, but with Christ in me, so that it is no longer I who live, but Christ who lives in me.

> For through the law I died to the law, so that I might live to God. I have been crucified with Christ; and it is no longer I who live, but

it is Christ who lives in me. And the life I now live in the flesh I live by faith in the Son of God, who loved me and gave himself for me. I do not nullify the grace of God; for if justification comes through the law, then Christ died for nothing (2:19-21).

Did Christ die *for you* for nothing? May it never be so! But I dare say, most of us are more like Cephas in his momentary lapses, than we are like Paul. Have you given the gospel, *the freedom of Christ,* full sway over you? Has the Prayer of Confession become for you your own public execution, with your own sin as Public Enemy Number One? Have you been crucified with Christ? If not, then have courage, courage to die to self, and do not wait another minute to begin practicing this daily discipline of which the apostle speaks when he says, "I die every day" (1Cor 15:31). Or, if you too have known and embraced this real, actual, existential death to sin, or if at least you are committed to living like a dead man walking, to standing as one who is slain, then is the freedom of Christ now the very thing that your whole life now signifies?

The Puritan pastor, Richard Baxter (1615-1691), once said, "I preached as never sure to preach again, and as a dying man to dying men." A stirring image, no doubt: one that this preacher and the person of faith would do well to imitate.

But the apostle sets a still higher standard, for the reality of his own death is no longer merely approaching. No. Even as it approaches in certainty, it has already come and gone, and he is absolutely free from it.

> I have been crucified with Christ; and it is no longer I who live, but it is Christ who lives in me. And the life I now live in the flesh I live by faith in the Son of God, who loved me and gave himself for me (2:19b-20).

Even our *grammar* exposes us! We say the *first* person singular pronoun is "I." "I" am the "first person, we say in our worldly way, and thus we are taught to "look out for number one!" But Christian faith has an altogether different grammar, such that "it is no longer 'I,' ... but Christ who lives in me."

Yes, eternal freedom begins at the cross, at the point where you no longer allow yourself any ground for arguing about who killed Jesus, whether or not he really lived and died, whether or not he was who he said he was. Your eternal freedom begins at the narrowest gate of all, the one where, in the present tense, you say for yourself and in the presence of the crucified God-man whose sovereignty is indisputable: "In the eyes of the law, I am a dead man, for I am a sinner, and I have no more hope of being proven innocent, for my own sin and the law itself accuse me. But I also know, O Lord Jesus, that you have arrived at the cross ahead of me, that you have endured it for me, that you have given up your life that I might be saved. Therefore, what can I give you in return? What have I to surrender, but I myself, my 'I,' my ego, that you might have room to make your home in me and with me. Thus, O Lord, consider me a living sacrifice, a sacrifice that is dead to sin and dead to self, but alive to you and in whom you may freely live."

Friend, this is the gospel of the freedom of Christ, the *eternal* freedom that consists in God's gracious relation to you. For when God looks at you, a sinner, a sinner who, having taken sanctuary *in Christ,* is now free, he does sees not sin, but he sees his obedient Son in whom you have your freedom, and he says, "You are my beloved Son! In you I am well-pleased." But when he sees you, as a new creation in Christ, a new creation with a whole new name, an adopted brother of Jesus, a brother who no longer asserts an "I," an *ego*, in the face of God, but who has said with the apostle in faith, "It is no longer 'I,' but Christ who lives in me," then God says to you, "Ah! I see the resemblance, I see my beloved Son in you, I see you have my Son in your heart, my Son with whom I am well pleased. Indeed, I hold him in my heart, too, and thus, as you love him;

yes, since you and I hold this love for my Son in common; yes, with you too am I well pleased; yes, I am well pleased. Now, be free! Now, my child, you are truly and eternally free."

Not Unity in Diversity, But Unity in Christ
(Galatians 3:1-21)

[Third Sunday of Lent, *February 13, 2005*]

PRAYER

O Holy Spirit, who inspired the prophets and the apostles in ages past, now inspire each listener, even as you fill and anoint your humble servant of the Word, that when I speak the word of Christ might be publicly proclaimed and heard, and where it is heard, faith might be born; and that, where there is faith, you might do your mighty works and be glorified. Yes, glorify yourself, O Holy God, glorify yourself and make us one, for you alone are one, and you alone are able to set us free to be one with you through Christ, in whose name, and in whose Spirit, we pray.

We live in an age that goes by the slogan: "unity in diversity." Or as our American currency says: *E pluribus unum* ["Out of many, one"]. As a nice bit of paradoxical ideology, it is fine, I suppose, in the political theory of earthly nations, but not in the kingdom of heaven, not where Christ is King.

It should be obvious, but where scriptural theology is overtaken by political theology, notice what happens. We read, "there is no longer Jew or Greek, ... there is no longer male or female," and then we proceed to draw up our particularistic ethno-centric interpretative approaches, feminist theologies, men's movements, and local theologies that have less to do with *theos* [God] and more to do with *anthropos* and *guné* [man and woman]. But three times the Spirit says, "no longer."[8] Just as we said last week: "It is no longer I, but Christ," here it is, "no longer Jew or Greek, no longer slave or free, no longer male or female, for all of you are one in Christ Jesus." The fact is, diversity as such does not have the means, the glue, so to speak, or even the willingness to suffer the pressure, the distress, or the sacrifice in order to produce the *coherence* that unity demands. But Christ, the suffering servant, the narrow gate, is one! The LORD your God is One! The Father and the Son and the Spirit are One!

---

[8] Slemmons, *Groans of the Spirit: Homiletical Dialectics in an Age of Confusion* (Eugene, OR: Pickwick Publications, 2010) p. 34, n. 109.

There is only one seed of Abraham who inherits the promise, only one through whom you too may grow up to share in this inheritance, and this one is not an abstract concept or ideology called diversity; it is a person whose name is Jesus.

The apostle goes to great lengths to make sure we understand that the noun in the position of the direct object in Genesis 13:15 is singular, not plural, when God says to Abraham, "for all the land that you see I will give to you and to your offspring forever," literally, to your *seed*, not to your *seeds*.

> Now the promises were made to Abraham and to his offspring; it does not say, "And to offsprings," as of many; but it says, "And to your offspring," that is, to one person, who is Christ (Gal 3:16).

The promise will come *through* Isaac and Jacob, *through* Judah and Tamar, *through* Jesse, *through* Ruth and Boaz, *through* David, *through* the line of kings, but it will come *to* Jesus Christ, the one and only seed, who will receive the fullness of the promise. "For in him all the fullness of God was pleased to dwell, and through him God was pleased to reconcile to himself all things, whether on earth or in heaven, by making peace through the blood of his cross" (Col 1:19-20). Yes, the One in whom the fullness of God was pleased to dwell, became, if I may put it this way, but a bare seed (1Cor 15:37), compressed in the olive press of Gethsemane.

We know from the synoptic parables of Matthew, Mark, and Luke that, "The seed is the word of God" (Luke 8:11; par.), from John, that Jesus is the Word of God (John 1:1-18), and from Paul, that Jesus is the seed of Abraham. From every angle, the one seed, and the singularity of the seed, the requisite unity that the world seeks and will never find in diversity, the unity it will never find until it bows before Christ as King—*the* unity is found *in* Christ alone.

So much hinges on that tiny preposition: *in*. For Paul, to be *in* Christ means, among other things, that we wear a whole new set of clothes.

Do you remember putting on your new Easter outfit every year? What was all that about? I tell you what it was all about.

> As many of you as were baptized into Christ have clothed yourselves with Christ. ... all of you are one in Christ Jesus (3:27, 28b).

> It is no longer I, but it is Christ who lives in me (2:20).

> And if you belong to Christ, then you are Abraham's offspring ... (3:29a);

you are the one seed, you (pl.) who are in Christ who have Christ as your head—you *are* Christ, *not instead* of Jesus, but because you are *in* him, you are part *of* him! Your identity *is* Christ!—and as members of the one heir, you are thus "heirs according to the promise" (3:29b).

Do you hear now, how, *if we are not in Christ, we are not one, and if we are not one, we are not in Christ?* Further, if we are not in Christ, if we are not one, we are not under grace but under the law, and therefore, under a curse. But in Christ, who became the curse for us, and who died, thus bringing an *end* to the curse and fulfillment to the purpose for which the law was given—in him we have every hope of being one, for he, the one seed, has said of himself:

> "Very truly, I tell you, unless a grain of wheat falls into the earth and dies, it remains just a single grain; but if it dies, it bears much fruit" (John 12:24).

Do you hear that? It is not: "Out of many, one." Our currency, our culture, and the whole world have it backwards! It is, rather: out of one, and that one being Christ, many are born; many are born who, in him, bear much fruit (John 15:5, 8). It is no coincidence that Paul will later, in Galatians 5, speak of fruit-bearing, contrasting the works of the flesh with the fruit of the Spirit (5:19-23); the very

Spirit the Galatians first received, not "by doing the works of the law," but "by believing what (they) heard" (3:2); the very Spirit who "worked *miracles* among (them), not by (their) doing the works of the law," but "by (their) *believing* what (they) heard" (3:5). So it is not "work, work, work." It is, rather,

> *breathe, believe, and grow;*
> *breathe, believe, and grow;*
> *breathe, believe, and grow.*

As the apostle says elsewhere, "So faith comes from what is heard, and what is heard comes through the word of Christ" (Rom 10:17). Faith comes so vividly when the word of Christ is heard and believed that Paul can say, as he reminds the Galatians of their first encounter with the gospel: "You foolish Galatians! Who has bewitched you? *It was before your eyes that Jesus Christ was publicly exhibited as crucified!*" Paul is not saying that the Galatians were eyewitnesses of the crucifixion some 20 years earlier. He is saying: When you heard it, you believed it, you received the Spirit, you saw miracles done among you, and at that very moment, *Jesus Christ was publicly exhibited as crucified*. That was the good news, the gospel of freedom that you received and believed.

Likewise, when the apostle writes to the Corinthians regarding the sacrament, which was being abused and ignored, the Spirit says: "as often as you eat this bread and drink the cup, you proclaim the Lord's death until he comes" (1Cor 11:26). In Corinthians, the word [*kataggellete*] means to *announce* or *make known*. In Galatians, it is to *prescribe* [*prografé*], to *write out ahead of time*, to *lay it out for all to see*. The gospel is no hidden, Gnostic, kabbalistic secret, known only to the elite insider. It is as wide open as the splayed arms of the crucified Christ, as stark and public as the cross against the sky. Yet, the Galatians had swooned. The freedom of Christ was too much for them. Their heads were dizzy as with a bad case of vertigo, and they retreated back under what they thought was the safety of the law. And they looked about as silly as a grown adult, trying to hide in the back row of a first grade classroom, sitting at a first grader's desk. They longed for their nanny, their child-minder, their tutor, their disciplinarian, their babysitter.

> Now before *faith* came, we *were* imprisoned and guarded under the law until faith would be revealed. Therefore the law was our *disciplinarian* until Christ came, so that we might be justified *by faith*. But *now that faith has come*, we are no longer subject to a disciplinarian, for *in Christ Jesus* you are all *children of God* through faith (3:23-26).

And when the Spirit of God calls you his children, he means you are his rightful heirs, through the one seed, the one rightful heir, the only one with any right to entitlement, Jesus Christ, yet who always defers obediently to the Father and the Spirit.

Yet, we are heirs, all the same. There is a will at stake. But unless we grow up, we will never have that appointment with the lawyer and the trustees of the estate, or the reading of the will, at which time the lawyer's job as trustee comes to an end, and the law, the will, is cancelled with it. For on that day it will be executed, just as Christ has been executed for our sakes.

The apostle is saying that the law, before Christ came, was the protector of the children, the security fence that kept us from running out into the street; the lawyer who administered the trust fund. It was also our teacher, our pedagogue, teaching us that, while we stand to inherit this great estate one day, when it comes, it will not come to us by any merit of ours, not because of our good grades, but because of the provident grace, the sheer goodness, the abundant love of our Father. The fact that we have been in the charge of a babysitter does not nullify the fact that we are children of our heavenly Father, or the fact that we are brothers and sisters to Christ our King, co-heirs, co-regents, of a vast, eternal kingdom, an enormous estate that we have not begun to explore.

But "if the inheritance comes from the law, it no longer comes from the promise; but God granted it to Abraham through the promise" (3:18). And as the apostle says elsewhere, "He who has prepared us for this very thing is God, who has given us the Spirit as a *guarantee*" (2Cor 5:5), a "deposit" [*NIV*], what the Reformers called the "earnest penny."

To entrust your salvation to yourself and to your own ability to earn it by doing works of the law, to gamble on the unlikely event that your own good works will one day so outweigh your bad ones that you will be able to demand salvation as an entitlement from the high and holy God—all of this is a terrible lapse from saving faith, a retreat from freedom, a refusal of the gospel, a rejection of Jesus and all that he has done for us. Paul asks,

> Having started with the Spirit, are you now ending with the flesh? (Gal 3:3b)

Have you not yet learned to trust God more than you trust yourself?

> Did you experience so much for nothing?— if it really was for nothing (3:4).

What we see here as the deadly danger of works righteousness has continued down through every generation of the Christian era. Augustine wrote against the heresy of Pelagianism, the Reformers against those who traded in indulgences, as though salvation could be bought or sold or earned. In every case, the heresy involves either forgetting or refusing to believe that God's grace is always at least one step ahead of us, indeed, that "he is able to do immeasurably more than all we ask or imagine" (Eph 3:20). It denies the fact that the best we can ever do is to *respond* to what God is *already* doing, thus it does away with grace as grace, freedom as freedom, the gospel as good news, unity as oneness, and Jesus as the Christ. It either intentionally denies, or implicitly refuses, all these things, as it tries to force God's hand to give what he is already trying to give anyway. But, ...

> Just as Abraham 'believed God, and it was reckoned to him as righteousness,' so, you see, those who believe are the descendants of Abraham. And the scripture, foreseeing that God would justify the Gentiles by faith, *declared the gospel beforehand* to Abraham, saying, 'All the Gentiles shall be blessed in you.' For this reason, those who believe are blessed with Abraham who believed. ... (So it is) that in Christ Jesus the blessing of

> Abraham (comes) to the Gentiles, so that we might receive the promise of the Spirit *through faith* (Gal 3:6-9, 14).

You have to believe in order to receive. It is as simple as that. Yet those obligatory words, "have to," must not, and those words too, "must not," must never, "and those words too, "must never," these words—how can I ever finish this sentence?—these words must never become a return to the law or be fashioned into a new work by which we earn what we cannot earn!

> Why then the law? It was added because of transgressions, until the seed (Jesus!) would come to whom *the promise* had been made ... For if a *law* had been given that could make alive, then righteousness would indeed come through *the law*. But *the scripture has imprisoned all things under the power of sin*, so that what was promised through faith in Jesus Christ might be given to those who believe (3:19-22).

The very writing of the Word of God both imprisons all things under the power of sin—*all things!*—and at the same time, arranges for an end to sin's tyranny. For when the living Word of God, Jesus Christ, was written out, publicly exposed— dashed like all our hopes of being found worthy on our own merits; dashed off like God's prescription—Jesus' death as a public exhibition declared our sickness (yours and mine and that of all the world, including those who bear the marks of baptism and who are thus now clothed with Christ) ... he declared our sickness and spelled out the necessary treatment, *all in one stroke*, all in one seed, all in one, *the* one, Jesus Christ, in whom *alone* the church will be found, and found as one.

Born According to the Spirit
(Galatians 4:1–5:1)

[Fourth Sunday of Lent, *March 6, 2005*]

PRAYER

O Lord, our God and Father, who in
the fullness of time sent forth your
Son, and sent him into our hearts to
cry unto you: hear our appeal that
we might now hear your reply, and
be lifted up in your presence, and
know the saving grace of your
countenance shining upon us and
the life of your Spirit stirring within
us, all for your glory!

Having compared the law to a *disciplinarian* or
pedagogue in Galatians 3, the apostle now says that,
as minors, we were once under a guardian, a
trustee, a steward, or a caretaker. By way of this
new analogy, however, he now implicitly
compares the law with something called the
stoicheia, from which we take the word *stoic*, or

43

stoicism. One of the Bible's most notoriously difficult words, *stoicheia* can be translated: the *basic principles of the world* (*NIV*), the *elements of the world* (*KJV*), *elemental things of the world* (*NASB*), the *ruling spirits of the universe* (*TEV*), the *elemental spirits* (or the *rudiments*) *of the world* (*NRSV*). Like the ABCs of reading, the notes of major scale in music, the primary numbers in mathematics, the four basic elements of pre-modern chemistry and physics (air, fire, earth, and water), the *stoicheia* in ancient pagan philosophy and religion were the base spirits behind astrology, the demigods of the pantheon. *Whatever* Paul means, whether one is copying the alphabet or counting on one hand, whether superstitiously seeking one's destiny in the stars or by watching things that go around come around again, either way, these *stoicheia* constitute the bars on one's cage. And what is really surprising is that, by drawing this analogy to the Hebrew law, or at least to the way in which certain Jewish legalists were applying it, he is really putting the law in its place. Among ancient religions, Judaism with its Torah was by far superior, but compared to the freedom of the children of God, the tendency of the law to devolve into legalism, the commandments to crystalize into monuments of stone, this tendency has more in common with the *stoicheia* of the pagans than with the kingdom of God.

Think, for instance, of the pagan worldview that says the world consists of those four basic elements. Now think how hard we work to purchase and maintain our quiet places in the country, complete with our clean-air machines; think how much we spend to heat our homes and keep the lights and the power on; think about what you pay for bottled water and water filters; think about how we work to put food on the table, the bounty of the earth. But Jesus has said,

> "do not worry, saying, 'What will we eat?' or 'What will we drink?' or 'What will we wear?' For it is the (pagans) who strive for all these things; and indeed your heavenly Father knows that you need all these things. But strive *first* for the kingdom of God and his righteousness, and all these things will be given to you as well" (Matt 6:31-33).

What is more, so that we will be encouraged to seek his kingdom first and foremost, God has even sent the Spirit of his Son into our hearts, crying, "Abba! Father!" God has given us his Spirit, as both our navigator and engine, to stir within us our proper longing for home, and he has given his Son that we might become his brothers, to become adopted children of the Father; he has given us Jesus to encourage us, saying, "Go ahead! Cry out to my Father! He is your Father, too, now! Call to him! You are welcome to call him Abba, too, if you like, or Papa, or Daddy, whatever you prefer, but call out to him, and just watch and wait and see how swiftly he will come scoop you up in his arms! See! You are no slave, you are a child of God and brother to your King!"

> Formerly, when you did not know God, you were enslaved to beings that by nature are not gods. Now ... that you have come to know God, or rather to be known by God, (surely you do not want to) turn back again to the weak and beggarly elemental spirits[!] (Surely you do not want to) be enslaved to them again[!] (Gal 4:8-9)

Put away your horoscopes, or use *them* as fire-starters on these cold winter days! For all the cyclical, seasonal, temporal observances have lost their meaning, all the clocks have gone haywire, all the quartz timers have been fried by the reality-altering pulse that has come with "the fullness of time," when "God sent his Son, born of a woman, born under the law, in order to redeem those who were under the law, ... that we might receive adoption" (4:4, 5).

Paul says, remember the good will you felt when we first met? The Galatians had welcomed him who had been mistreated for the gospel he preached, welcomed him "as an angel of God, as Christ Jesus" (4:14). And they had welcomed his message. He says,

> You have done me no wrong. ... (But), had it been possible, you would have torn out your eyes and given them to me. Have I now become your enemy by telling you the truth? (4:12b, 15b-16)

Then he employs this strange metaphor, saying that he, an apostle of the church, is, in a sense, their mother:

> My little children, for whom I am again in the pain of childbirth until Christ is formed in you, I wish I were present with you now and could change my tone, for I am perplexed about you (4:19-20).

Here he thought that faith had been born in them, that the indwelling Christ had taken up residence in them, that each one could then say, "It is no longer I, but Christ," but apparently the baby had scrambled back inside. They had retreated from faith and thus from freedom. Now Paul is back in the delivery room, travailing in labor until faith be formed anew; and what is more, he says: "Become as I am," ... do not retreat from faith and freedom, but give yourself to the

47

task of helping faith, helping Christ, be born in others! One hears the strains of the letter to the Hebrews: "For though by this time you ought to be teachers, you need someone to teach you again the basic elements (the *stoicheia*) of the oracles of God. You need milk, not solid food" (Heb 5:12). The difference is, that the Hebrews had forgotten the very purpose of the law, the basics of the basics: you learn your ABC's so that you can read and communicate with God as his children; whereas the Galatians, in trying to take on the yoke of the Jewish laws and customs, were forgetting that they had *already* been made children, had come into a great inheritance, yet they thought it too good to be true.

Surely it could not be this simple. Surely we must first meet the requirements that God set forth for his chosen people Israel. We must follow their laws, their calendar, their customs. But the apostle says, No. "Tell me, you who desire to be subject to the law, will you not listen to the law? For it is *written* ..." (4:21-22a), he says, and from the Torah, he recalls the history of Abraham's two sons, Ishmael and Isaac, born to a slave woman, Hagar, and to Sarah, his wife, respectively. "One, the child of the slave, was born according to the flesh; the other, the child of the free woman, was born through the promise" (4:23). On the one side of this allegory, there is the covenant of the law, written on stone, given at Sinai, the earthly Jerusalem, and all of this corresponds to slavery, to Hagar, the fertile slave, and her son Ishmael, of whom the angel said, "He shall be a wild ass of a man, with his hand against everyone, and everyone's hand against him; and he shall live at odds with all his kin" (Gen 16:12). On the other hand, there is Sarah, the beloved and barren wife, corresponding to the new Jerusalem, coming down from heaven above; "she is free, and she is our mother. For it is written" (4:26b-27a),

> Sing, O barren one, who did not bear;
> burst into song and shout,
> you who have not been in labor!
> For the children of the desolate woman
> will be more than the children of the
> one who is married,
> says the LORD (Isa 54:1; cf. Gal 4:27b).

Does this not now contradict everything we have just said? Was not Sarah the married one, and Hagar unmarried? Yes, but until Isaac, who is here called the child *born according to the Spirit*, Sarah was childless, desolate, and experienced no birth pangs. More importantly, for us, Paul applies this allegory to the church:

> Now you, my friends, are children of the
> promise, like Isaac. ... So then, friends, we

are children, not of the slave but of the free woman. For freedom Christ has set us free. Stand firm, therefore, and do not submit again to a yoke of slavery (4:28, 31—5:1).

In the Apostles' Creed we say that, Jesus Christ, the Son of God, was *conceived by the Holy Ghost*, the Holy Spirit, and born of the Virgin Mary. But here, Paul likens us to Isaac, whose father, like the Father of Jesus, also laid wood on his back and offered him as a sacrifice on Mt. Moriah; he likens us to Isaac, the child of the promise, the child of freedom, so that the sacrifice of Jesus, and that of Isaac, were sacrifices freely made; he likens us to Isaac, who is also called the one born according to the Spirit. Yes, the Spirit, speaking through the apostle, says to us, you too are born according to the Spirit, you too, though you came body and soul into this world, born ... of blood and of the will of the flesh and of the will of your human father and mother, ... now you too must be born of the will of God, conceived (if you will) by the Holy Ghost. This is why Jesus said to Nicodemus: "What is born of the flesh is flesh, what is born of the Spirit is spirit. Do not be astonished that I said to you, 'You must be born from above.' The wind blows where it chooses, and you hear the sound of it, but you do not know where it comes from or where it goes. So it is with everyone who is born of the Spirit" (John 3:6-8). "Very truly, I tell you, no one can see the kingdom of God without being born from above" (John 3:3).

What is surprising is that Paul says the Galatians, for whom he is once again suffering birth pangs, the Galatians about whom he is most perplexed, are already children of freedom, but they are not acting like it. This is why he also warns that, according to rabbinic tradition, Ishmael, the wild ass, persecuted Isaac of the promise. For "the child who was born (only) according to the flesh persecuted the child who was born according to the Spirit, ... and so it is now also" (4:29). *So it is also now!* ... for the Galatians when they read this, and for us today.

But who is Ishmael here and who is Isaac? Who is the slave child and who is the free? I say, as long as we must labor under the burden of this mortal flesh, we are all both! I say, even though Jesus himself said, "No one can serve two masters; ... You cannot serve God and wealth" (Matt 6:24), we try to do it anyway! It is not possible to serve two masters, yet we persist! Therefore, in God's eyes, we are *impossible!* Yearning for the world, yet struggling to shed our fleshliness, to be born out of the world and into the freedom of the kingdom of God, all by the heaving labor pangs of the apostolic church, a church that itself sometimes seems to have given up its apostolic calling. And I do not mean just the mainline or just the evangelical churches; I mean the whole lot of us, regardless of our annual reports, our esthetic styles, or the ethical relevance of our worship.

And yet, we are neither Ishmael nor Isaac. No, we are rather, every one of us, more like Isaac's wife Rebekah, who has two nations at war within her womb: Esau, a rash, foolish, stubborn ass; and Jacob, tenacious, grasping at his brother's heel, yet, seeking a blessing from God.

> But what does the scripture say? "Drive out the slave and her child; for the child of the slave will not share the inheritance with the child of the free woman" (4:30).

So drive out the rash, the foolish, the worldly, the wild ass from your mind, your heart, your motives, your desires! Ishmael and Esau have no more spirit than the rock hard tablets of the law. They talk of Fate, as they are yanked about on chains by the elemental spirits" of the universe. Nearly 4000 years old, and they have not yet begun to learn their ABC's! Neither have the pagan astrologers and philosophers, seeking only what they will eat and drink and wear and be entertained by. But as Pascal said, it is "*not* the God of the philosophers, but the God of Abraham, Isaac, and Jacob!"

> "Drive out the slave and her child; for the child of the slave will not share the inheritance with the child of the free woman." ... For freedom Christ has set us free. Stand firm, therefore, and do not submit again to a yoke of slavery! (4:30; 5:1)

What is the yoke that entices you to shoulder it again and again? What is the millstone that grinds you under its weight? Is it fear, anger, bitterness, or pride? Is it an old wound, a forged identity, a moment of shame that has destroyed your self-esteem? Is it something that consumes your time, your energy, your money, your thoughts, your affections? Is it a habit, a substance, a website, a device, a nightmare? Is it your property, your diet, your perfectionism? Has some form of amnesia papered over your dearest hopes, your most important dreams? Whatever it is that menaces you every time your thoughts rise in hope of the true and eternal freedom for which Christ has set you free, let it go. Tell it: "No." Tell it: "I will no longer submit to you, because my brother Jesus, has set me free, and he has something better in mind for me! Yes, for freedom Christ has set me free!"

The Only Thing That Counts
(Galatians 5:1-26)

[Fifth Sunday of Lent, *March 13, 2005*]

PRAYER

O Lord our God, you who desire the fruit of the Spirit, who inspired the apostles with your Spirit, guide us now as we consider the Scriptures that you have inspired. May my speaking and our hearing likewise be inspired, that we may understand and live so as to inspire others to seek and follow Christ without stumbling.

Yes, you heard that right. The apostle says it would be better if those who had tripped up the Galatian church by insisting the men undergo circumcision would go all the way and castrate themselves. *What is that all about?* Does he mean

55

this literally, metaphorically, earnestly, or ironically? Is this a curse of some kind, or an inspired bit of asceticism?

First of all, Paul is not thinking of the pediatric procedure performed on male infants for the reasons it is done today; neither is he writing to little Jewish boys who are only seven days old, as though they were capable of deciding such matters for themselves before the eighth day! He is talking very specifically to Gentile-background converts to Christianity who, confused by a false teaching that was going around, were considering undergoing this cosmetic surgery as a form of religious initiation into Judaism—to life under the law!—in hopes that this religious ceremony would bring them the covenant benefits of God's relation to the Jews. "Once again I testify to every *man* (!) who lets himself be circumcised that he is obliged to obey the entire law" (5:3). What is at stake is not ultimately the question of whether to circumcise or not to circumcise, but *that* question has begged the greater question regarding the purpose of the law: *Of what benefit is the law?* And *that* question in turn has begged the even *greater* question: Why do we need Christ? Or as Anselm of Canterbury put it: *Cur Deus Homo? Why the God-Man?*

The big red question mark from the *Alpha* course is not about a little bit of skin, or (for those who know the Dr. Seuss book) whether you are a star-bellied or a non-star-bellied Sneetch. Still less is it about doing our little bit to show the world what good little boys and girls we are. "*Why do we need the God-Man?*" is an infinitely greater question that that!

Surely you see now why Paul likens the law to the *stoicheia*, to the weak and beggarly spirits (4:9), since all these things can do is beg bigger and bigger questions; questions that the law itself cannot address; questions to which Christ alone is the answer! "Listen! I, Paul, am telling you that if you let yourselves be circumcised"—if you choose the law as your means of being justified before God; if you think you will be able to live up to the absolute demands of the law; if you think you are able to amass enough gold stars or extra credits for obedience and good works to convince God that you are perfect, so that he will be forced to give you what he already has given you in Christ, then—"Christ will be of no benefit to you. ... You who want to be justified by the law have cut yourselves off from Christ; you have fallen away from grace" (5:2, 4). The greatest abuse of grace, the way to "outrage the spirit of grace" (Heb 10:29), is to reject grace altogether; it is to allow sin to tell you what to do, rather than you learning to tell sin and temptation where they can go.

As the LORD said to Cain, who had become angry: "sin is lurking at the door; its desire is for you, but you must master it" (Gen 4:7). As Jesus said: "everyone who commits sin is a slave to sin; ... but if the Son makes you free, you will be free indeed" (John 8:34-35). The question is, where sin is concerned, will you be a slave of sin or will you become its master and commander? Will you, with the authority of the children of God, command sin to be silent, to be still, to go away? It is the one who is *in* Christ Jesus the Son of God who is, *with* him, a child of God. It is the one who is in faith who is truly free, free to drive sin and temptation out of the heart and out of the house, out of the mind and out of the neighborhood; to banish it from its master's presence. And when sin comes skulking back and lurks at the door, waiting for an opportune moment, how will *the new you* respond—you who are no longer a slave cowering under the law, but a child of God; you who now share in the administration of righteousness; who now has a stake in the family inheritance? You who are wary of sin and wise to its ways; you who see through the tricks of the tempter; who know that "a little yeast leavens the whole batch of dough" (5:9); who remain on guard, faithfully in Christ Jesus, "obeying the truth" (5:7); you who know that Christ Jesus *is* the Truth, in whom "neither circumcision nor uncircumcision counts for anything ..." (5:6a)? Yes, if you think through the metaphor, Paul is saying that the whole circumcision question is but a smokescreen behind which those who are offended at Christ try to remove the scandal, the sheer, naked embarrassment, of the cross. Yet, the cross of Christ is the gospel itself:

> the message about the cross is foolishness to those who are perishing, but to us who are being saved it is the power of God. ... For Jews demand signs and Greeks desire wisdom, but we proclaim *Christ crucified*, a stumbling block [a *scandal*, an *offense*] to Jews and foolishness to Gentiles, but to those who are the called, both Jews and Greeks, Christ the power of God and the wisdom of God. For God's foolishness is wiser than human wisdom, and God's weakness is stronger than human strength (1Cor 1:18, 22-25).

The Spirit says, *let anything* that would obscure the gospel: every smokescreen, every circumcision or sexuality debate, every obsession [or *idée fixe*], every exaltation of sin, every argument based on human wisdom and persuasion [*peismone*]—"such persuasion does not come from the one who calls you!" (5:8)—every ecclesial foray into international diplomacy, every lapse into objectivism, artifice, or juridical trivia *be cut off*, so that all these means of avoiding the cross would be emasculated, and those who take offense at the God-man, the crucified Christ, would become as the apostle is (4:12): a eunuch for the kingdom of heaven (Matt 19:12; 1Cor 7:8). And *no*, he does *not* mean *literally*, but spiritually.

Like Jesus cursing of the fig tree that was all leaves and no fruit, no good for nourishment, but useful only for designing fig leaf loin-cloths to hide our nakedness from God—"May no one ever eat fruit from you again!" (Mark 11:12-14)—so the apostle is saying of those who would trip you when you are running well, to those who would confuse you by removing the offense of the cross: "they will pay the penalty" (Gal 5:10). They would be better off *not only* having a bit of skin removed, the foreskin that is the focus of all their fixations, but going all the way, and having every distraction from and every way of dissolving the cross and its gospel cut off. No, it is the crucified Christ, the Atonement for sin publicly nailed to the cross that exposes sin as well as the sinner, and there are only two possible responses to our being thus exposed. *One* response, the one that misses the blessing he offers (Matt 11:6), is to be offended at him: "Who is this Jesus that he thinks he can expose my sin and me as a sinner? Who is he to think that he can die for me, as though I need him? There are plenty of other ways to heaven, surely, than this embarrassing public spectacle!" *The other* response, the blessed one, the one I hope and trust you have made and will continue to make, is the response of *faith* as confession, *faith* as repentance. And, now that you are thoroughly convicted of sin, thoroughly convicted of the Truth, *faith* as that which is now absolutely opposed to sin, to sin as faith's opposite (Rom 14:23), faith that is now the only thing that matters: "the only thing that counts is faith working through love" (Gal 5:6b).

> For you were called to freedom … ; only do not use your freedom as an opportunity for self-indulgence, but through love become slaves to one another. For the whole law is summed up in a single commandment, "You shall love your neighbor as yourself." (5:13-14)

Only the one who, in Christ, *in faith*, has mastered and is completely opposed to sin, … only that one has enough mastery over the self—precisely because the master of the self is the Servant King, Jesus Christ—to willingly become a slave to one's brothers and sisters in Christ. This is the Spirit in which, in whom, Jesus himself, "although he was a Son, … learned obedience through suffering" (Heb 5:8), the Spirit in whom Jesus himself, "though he was in the form of God, did not regard equality with God as something to be exploited, but emptied himself, taking the form of a slave, … humbled himself, and became obedient to the point of death, even death on a cross" (Phil 2:6-8). This is the Spirit, the Holy Spirit, of whom the apostle speaks when he says, "Let the same mind be in you that was in Christ Jesus" (2:5). For when you live by this Spirit, you do not "gratify the desires of the flesh" (Gal 5:16). When you are "led by the Spirit, you are not subject to the law" (5:18), but you are royal subjects of Christ your King, your brother who suffered and died for you; your Savior, the best and only friend of your eternal freedom; the One to whom you owe your absolute allegiance!

Here it is, my friend: life's great *either/or!* For the Bible says: "if we live by the Spirit, let us also be guided by the Spirit" (Gal 5:25). But "what the flesh desires is opposed to the Spirit, and what the Spirit desires is opposed to the flesh; for these are opposed to each other, to prevent you from doing what you want" (5:17). "Now the works of the flesh are obvious: fornication, impurity, licentiousness, idolatry, sorcery, enmities, strife, jealousy, anger, quarrels, dissensions, factions, envy, drunkenness, carousing, and things like these" (5:19-21a). But "those who belong to Christ Jesus have crucified the flesh with its passions and desires" (5:24). And we have been warned: "those who," instead of crucifying these things, entertain and indulge them, those who "*do* such things will not inherit the kingdom of God" (5:21).

On the other hand, in the final analysis, life's great *either/or* offers us no real choice at all. For who can compare life and death, as though they were of equal value? Compared to the law, the works of the flesh, and the slavery to sin, the fruit of the Spirit is of such a superior quality—not only of life, but of *holy, eternal* life—that there really is no comparison at all. There is no choice to speak of. The only alternative to life is a trap, a delusion, a deadly deception.

Now, there will doubtless be many who prefer to hide in their fig trees, who seek to maintain the illusion as long as they can, who will exercise the disastrous "choice" for the *Either* rather than the *Or*, for slavery to sin, rather than the freedom of Christ. But having chosen slavery, does one then find oneself *enjoying* the benefits of a free choice? By no means! To abandon freedom in Christ and return to the yoke of slavery: *that* is no free choice! It is a choice only one who prefers misery and prison would make, one who has never stood upright and freely mastered sin.

But for the one who takes no offense at the cross; who, in utter conviction, *clings* to the cross and abides in the One who was crucified upon it; for the one who abides and discovers a whole new identity in the One on whom the Spirit descended and remained; for the one who responds in faith, stands firm against sin, and banishes sin from one's new Christ-like existence, that one—*you!*—will bear the incomparable fruit of the Spirit, the fruit that testifies, not to a cosmetic or a legalistic circumcision, but to a faith within, the circumcised heart of which Moses (Deut 30:6) and Jeremiah (6:10; 9:25-26) and Paul (Rom 2:29) all spoke. "By contrast (to the old ways of the flesh), the fruit of the Spirit" ... the fruit of *faith* ... "is (*first*) love, (*then*) joy, peace, patience, kindness, generosity, faithfulness, gentleness, and self-control. There is no law against such things" (Gal 5:22-23), no law that can succeed in either opposing or in bringing about such things.

"No, the only thing that counts"—*the only thing!*—"is faith working *through* love" (5:6b)—*through* love!—to produce all this other "produce" of the Spirit!

Compared to these things, what choice is there, really? Is there, for the person of faith, an either/or? No, there is no *either/or*; there is only a *from/to*; a calling away from slavery and sin, a summoning away from flesh and fetish. There is only a homecoming to faith and freedom, to a qualitative change in your inner being that allows you to be both a child with respect to God and a mature master with respect to sin; both a servant with respect to the needs of your fellow citizens in the kingdom, and an heir apparent to royal responsibility by virtue of your kinship to your brother Jesus Christ, "the King of kings and Lord of lords" (1Tim 6:16; Rev 19:16).

Come away, then, *from* the fruitless works of the flesh; from slavery to sin, which is less than nothing. *Come away to* the freedom of Christ: to freedom in the Spirit, to the only thing that counts, to faith working through love, to a free and fruitful life in eternity, to a life in eternal love. *Come away*, says the Christ. *Come away*, says, the Spirit. *Come away*, says the Beloved, to you who— once a sinner, now a spirit—keep your soul in purity and faithfulness to him. No, the law cannot speak to you in this way. Only the Bridegroom of your soul can say:

> "Arise, my love, my fair one,
> and come away;
> for now the winter is past,
> the rain is over and gone.
> The flowers appear on the earth;
> the time of singing has come,
> and the voice of the turtledove
> is heard in our land.
> The fig tree *puts* forth its figs,
> and the vines are in blossom;
> they give forth fragrance.
>
> Arise, my love, my fair one,
> and come away.

O my dove, in the clefts of the rock,
in the covert of the cliff,
let me see your face,
let me hear your voice;
for your voice is sweet,
and your face is lovely"
(Song 2:10-14).

Everything!
(Galatians 6:1-18)

[Sixth Sunday of Lent (Palm/Passion), *March 20, 2005*]

PRAYER

Eternal God, you who have placed the cross of Jesus Christ squarely between the old and the new, between flesh and spirit, between the law of stone and the gospel of freedom: how blessed are those who take no offense at you! In this hour, O God, and in the grace of your Spirit, help each one here to seek you in humility, to test his or her own work, to find joy in the discovery that we share in all good things with you, our true Teacher, and to experience in the cross everything needful, a new creation—*everything!*—so that we might never grow weary in doing what is right, in Jesus' name.

Not *Either/Or*, but *From/To*. That is the dialectic of repentance and faith. We are called *from* works of the flesh *to* bearing the fruit of the Spirit. The apostle says: "My friends" (6:1a)—after all his passionate polemics, the Galatians are still his friends, literally, his *brothers*—"if anyone is detected in a transgression" (6:1b), that is, if anyone is *clearly* engaged in those *obvious* works of the flesh: "fornication, impurity, licentiousness, idolatry, sorcery, enmities, strife, jealousy, anger, quarrels, dissensions, factions, envy, drunkenness, carousing, and things like these" (5:19-21), "you who have received the Spirit should restore such a one in a spirit of gentleness" (6:1c), *gentleness*, of course, being one of the spiritual fruits!

What is more, for all the absolutely stark differences between fleshly works and spiritual fruit, which seem as far apart as light and darkness, heaven and hell, nevertheless, these opposites are still close enough to warrant this warning: "Take care that you yourselves are not tempted" (6:1d), and they are still close enough to make it possible for us to "Bear one another's burdens, and in this way ... fulfill the law of Christ" (6:2), the law of Christ being that we should "love one another," for love itself "is the fulfilling of the law" (Rom 13:10).

Our earthly journey, the whole of life, is fraught with danger, the danger of sin lurking at the door (Gen 4:7) and evil lying so very close at hand (Rom 7:21), so close that, when we try to help another, we must take care not to fall into the same trap.

So much of the time, those who are in the grip of sin want company in their sin! You have heard it said that "misery loves company," but I say to you, sin wants it even more! It is one thing to show compassion by weeping with those who weep (Rom 12:15), as we should do; by bearing one another's burdens—these are good things, so if misery loves company, it is surely loving to sit with someone who is miserable and be miserable with them for a while. We do it for one another in hospital waiting rooms and funeral homes. But it is another thing altogether, when the cause of someone's misery is sin, to *join* them in the sin. There is nothing loving about that, neither loving toward the neighbor, nor loving toward oneself, nor loving toward God; such a contagion only compounds the damage and hurts everyone all around.

The humble way is, knowing that I am nothing, to remain nothing in my own eyes, and thereby to remain in the truth—the truth that is love—to remain undeceived. "For if those who are nothing think they are something, they deceive themselves" (6:3). The deadly trap, to be avoided at all costs, is the trap one falls into when one compares oneself to another (2Cor 10:12). It really does not matter whether one looks *up* at someone who, in one's own eyes, makes one look *bad*, or whether one looks *down* on someone who, in the eyes of the ego, makes one look *good*. Either way, such a person only stokes the ego, whether with indignation and resentment, or pride and superiority. Either way, comparing oneself with others in but a futile attempt to avoid the only thing that counts, to avoid faith working through love, to avoid becoming conscious of one's own sin, to avoid it by taking offense at the way in which Christ's exposure on the cross exposes the self as a sinner (Kierkegaard). For to focus on another's sin is only a way of avoiding consciousness of one's own. Comparing yourself to another is only ever a way of stepping away from the reflection that the Son of God, hanging rejected on the cross, casts back into your own life. This is why the apostle says,

> All must test their own work; then that work, rather than their neighbor's work, will become a cause for pride. For all must carry their own loads (6:4).

Yes, each of us must carry our own loads, as each of us bear our crosses, yoked as we are with

Christ; yet, in relation to others, the proper attitude is not to draw comparisons at all, but to adopt a spirit of gentleness, kindness, and understanding, to help one another bear each other's particular, incomparable burdens. There is no contradiction in what Paul says, not if I remember that I am nothing, for if I am nothing, then I have nothing of my own that will serve as a basis for comparing myself with my brother or sister, and therefore, nothing against which he or she will seem either intimidating or despicable to me.

No, I am nothing. But a new creation is everything, and it is in Christ that one discovers one *is* a new creation! "It is no longer I who live, but it is Christ who lives in me!" (2:20)

Think, for instance, of the sons of Noah: Shem, Ham, and Japheth. After surviving the flood, dear old Noah—and Noah was *old!*—dear old Noah planted a vineyard, got drunk, and lay around drunk and naked in his tent (Gen 9:18-21). Ham, seeing that his father was naked, "told his two brothers outside" (9:21). It hardly seems like a big deal. It was not as if, after the flood, there was anyone else to see or hear the news that Ham, the original tabloid, blurted out before the whole newly scrubbed creation: *Hey, guys! Guess what I just saw!*

71

But Shem and Japheth, in a spirit of gentleness, in a spirit of humility, respect, and discretion, with the attitude of those who knew that they too were, in the words of the risen Jesus to the Laodiceans (Rev 3:17), "wretched, pitiable, poor, blind, and naked" before the eyes of heaven;" who knew that they too, in the aftermath of the flood that destroyed every other living thing on the face of the earth, they too might have been tempted to take just a bit too much wine: "Shem and Japheth took a garment, laid it on both their shoulders, and walked backward and covered the nakedness of their father; their faces were turned away, and they did not see their father's nakedness" (Gen 9:23). And when Noah woke up, it was Shem and Japheth whom he blessed, and it was Canaan, the son of Ham, whom he cursed (9:24-25). No ogling, no voyeurism, no mockery, nothing like that for the humble, but only discretion, gentleness, a respectful bearing of the other's burden, a doing for the old man what, in his present state, he was not able to do for himself.

> Do not be deceived; God is not mocked, for you reap whatever you sow. If you sow to your own flesh, you will reap corruption from the flesh; but if you sow to the Spirit, you will reap eternal life from the Spirit. So let us not grow weary in doing what is right, for we will reap at harvest-time, if we do not

give up. So then, whenever we have an opportunity, let us work for the good of all, and especially for those of the family of faith (Gal 6:7-10).

How many of you know what it is like to care for the elderly and infirm, or for newborn children, who cannot care for themselves? Many, if not most of you, know this responsibility very well, and the Lord will not forget it. For the One who remembers every cup of cold water given (Mark 9:41) will not forget what you have done to preserve another's dignity. Do not give up! But "work for the good of *all*, ... *especially* for those of the household of faith!" (Gal 6:10)

Why should we *not* give up? What is it that makes the indignity, the shame, the humiliation of life, worth putting up with? As Paul exclaimed to the Romans: "Wretched man that I am! Who will rescue me from this body of death? Thanks be to God through Jesus Christ our Lord!" (Rom 7:24-25) And to the Philippians, "He (Christ) will transform the body of our humiliation that it may be conformed to the body of his glory, by the power that also enables him to make all things subject to himself" (Phil 3:21). Paul, who came to the Galatians and was received by them as though he were Jesus Christ himself; Paul, who first announced the gospel to them because of his own physical infirmity, a condition that put them to the test (Gal 4:13), yet they did not despise him; Paul, who testifies here that he carries "the marks of Jesus branded on (his) body" (6:17)—Paul knows that life in the body is utterly embarrassing, far more embarrassing than a hospital gown, and he speaks of the body as the "body of death," "the body of our humiliation." He knows that, whether we are blessed with energy, health, vim and vigor, a fetching smile, straight teeth, luxurious hair, a nice figure, the fact is that, try as we might, it will not last.

> "The grass withers, the flower fades,
>> when the breath of the LORD blows
>> upon it; surely the people are grass.
> The grass withers, the flower fades;
>> but the word of our God will stand
>> forever" (Isa 40:7-8).

To the Corinthians the apostle writes, "the present form of this world is passing away" (1Cor 7:31); and to the Galatians,

> It is those who want to make a good showing in the flesh that try to compel you to be circumcised—only that they may not be persecuted for the cross of Christ (6:12).

"... *only that they may not be persecuted for the cross of Christ.*" Those who live for the sake of "keeping up appearances," like Hyacinth Bou-*quet*, will stop at nothing to flee the eternal light that shines from the cross on which you and I and they and every other human under heaven once crucified the Son of God. For those who take offense at the cross and its good news, the cross with its *From/To* reorienting power; for those for whom there is neither *From* nor *To*, but only this present *pretense* of permanence—for such as these it is all about boasting in the flesh of possessions, aspirations, experiences, externals; it is all about zooming past God's living, loving relational promise to Abraham and crashing headlong into tablets of stone.

> Even the circumcised do not themselves obey the law, but they want you to be circumcised so that they may boast about your flesh (6:13).

But, Paul says,

> May I never boast of anything except the cross of our Lord Jesus Christ, by which the world has been crucified to me, and I to the world. For neither circumcision nor uncircumcision is anything; but a new creation is everything! (6:14-15)

Everything! A new creation is everything! A new Genesis! A new tree of life! A new fruit, the fruit of the Spirit, of which all are invited to partake! But it is a fruit that can be found on no other tree, none other than the very cross on which Christ has died, the very cross on which flesh and sin, transgression and temporality, *die*, and I die to them ... only to be reborn!

Yes, the reason Jerusalem cheered Jesus on Sunday, and jeered and denied and crucified him on Friday; the reason the world rejected him so, was not for expectations too high, but too low. We wanted a conquering hero, a dashing, winsome golden boy to win a political victory. It never occurred to this dying creation that death itself and sin were doomed, that the devil himself, and all of his realm, the nether-regions of rebellion and the very heart of darkness and depravity, were trained in the sights, in the crosshairs of the cross. It never occurred to this stupid world that the one who gave himself to *this* death, on *this* day, was giving meaning to the death, to the dying of the whole decrepit, decaying order of creation, and bringing a whole new creation into being, a whole new sinless Adam.

But this, my friends, is everything! A new creation ... *everything!* "So if *anyone* is in Christ, there is a new creation: everything old has passed away; see, everything has become new!" (2Cor

5:17). "See," says Jesus, "I am making all things new. ... Write this, for (my) words are trustworthy and true" (Rev 21:5). All you need to do, is step in, step over the threshold of gospel faith and freedom, look up to the pierced side of Christ, slip inside and take shelter in him. Look up to him, cry out to him, and *voila! New creation!* This is everything. *Everything!*

I know full well, and I often counsel preaching students, that the preacher should never attempt to say everything in a single sermon. But—God, help me—as the apostle has written in the Spirit, so have I have tried in that same Spirit to say *everything!*

> May the grace of our Lord Jesus Christ be with your spirit ... Amen (6:18).

About the Author

TIMOTHY MATTHEW SLEMMONS is *Associate Professor of Homiletics and Worship* at the University of Dubuque Theological Seminary. A Presbyterian teaching elder, he has served churches in Pennsylvania and New Jersey, and preached as far afield as Jamaica, Scotland, and Malawi. A past recipient of the David H. C. Read Preacher/Scholar Award (1994), his publications include *Groans of the Spirit: Homiletical Dialectics in an Age of Confusion* (2010); *Year D: A Quadrennial Supplement to the Revised Common Lectionary* (2012), and the 4-volume series, *Liturgical Elements for Reformed Worship* (2013-14).

Made in the USA
Columbia, SC
19 April 2019